AUSTR

TRAVEL JOURNAL

UNPLUG & WRITE

WANDERLUST JOURNALS COLLECTION

WWW.WANDERLUST-JOURNALS.COM

INDEX

WANDERLUST

The term originates from the German words wandern (to hike) and Lust (desire).
The word in English occurred in 18th century as a reflection of what was then seen as a characteristically German predilection for wandering.

In modern German, the use of the word Wanderlust is less common, having been replaced by Fernweh (lit. "farsickness"), coined as an antonym to Heimweh ("homesickness").
Wanderlust is the intense urge for self-development by experiencing the unknown, confronting unforeseen challenges, getting to know unfamiliar cultures, ways of life and behaviours.

WHEN WE TRAVEL

WE STOP BEING WHO WE ARE

TO BECOME BEING

WHO WE WANT TO BE.

BY AIR MAIL

AUG
7 PM

WHAT IS TO TRAVEL?

When we travel, we move along distance and time, between two different points.

Etymology

The first known word use was in the 14th century. The word "travel" may originate from the Old French which means to work strenuously. The origin of the word reflects the extreme difficulty of travel in ancient times. Even though today it is easier to travel, we are used to travel hurriedly. We are used to follow the masses and to do what everyone tells us to do. This book, suggests ways to make a pause and contemplate details, and motivates us to write down all our thoughts.

25 GREAT REASONS TO TRAVEL

Some people say we travel only for two reasons,
- either to escape from something
- or to look for something new.

But there are more reasons.

1. Travel is to leave the beaten path

2. Travel is opening wounds, so then the sun can heal them

3. Travel gives us an excuse to learn a new language.

4. Travel is open the door to the unconscious memories

5. Travel makes us rethink stereotypes.

6. Travel is to convert the lack of Wifi in the possibility of looking into the eyes of those who are travelling with you

7. Travel makes us believe in the kindness of strangers.

8. Travel is to leave all the excuses at home

9. Travel is to expand our tolerance

10. Travel makes it okay not to fit in

11. Travel gives us the opportunity to start from scratch

12. Travel makes us remove the autopilot with which we drive our lives

13. Travel makes us vulnerable

14. Travel is to reinvent ourselves

15. Travel makes us to be friends of strangers

16. Travel is to get lost to finally find with anyone else but ourselves

17. Travel makes us do crazy things

18. Travel is like jumping from stone to stone the river of life. Where every stone are the trips we have done, and the river flowing, our daily lives

19. Travel makes us enjoy discomfort

20. Travel makes us appreciate home

21. Travel is a panacea

WHAT ARE THE REASONS WHY I TRAVEL?

22.   ...

23.   ...

24.   ...

25.   ...

TRAVEL IS PURE INSPIRATION

The word inspiration comes from the Latin word "inspiratio", inspiration is the process on which outside air enters the lungs and promotes thoughts in the mind.

In Greek thought, inspiration meant that the artist would go into ecstasy. It was the figure of the muse that was considered to be the goddess who "carried" the artists to perform their different jobs.

Life begins with an inspiration, and when life itself expires, it does so with an exhalation.

This trip is my inspiration.

IF FOUND

PLEASE RETURN IT TO:

NAME:

ADDRESS:

PHONE NUMBER:

EMAIL ADDRESS:

TRIP PLANNER

W?

What? (Do I want to learn from this trip)

_____

_____

When? (Do I travel?)

_____

_____

Where? (Do I go?)

_____

_____

Why? (Do I travel?)

_____

_____

CHECKLIST

THINGS TO DO BEFORE LEAVING

Family and Friends

Telephone numbers

(in case I lose my phone)

Packing list

Things I'm taking with me

Carry-on
Important Documents and Necessities

Hygiene and medicine

CLOTHING

MISCELLANEOUS

Itinerary Overview

MAPS

(Paste map)

My favourite landscapes

My favourite museums

Restaurants I love

My chillout places

SERENDIPITOUS TRAVEL MOMENTS:

Serendipity is an unexpected discovery when we are seeking something different.

The word emerged in 1700 from a Persian fairy tale, which takes place on an island called "Serendip", in which the protagonists solved all their problems through coincidences.

WHAT IS MY SERENDIPITOUS MOMENT IN THIS TRIP?

Things I do while traveling but not at home:

SONGS THAT INSPIRE ME ON THIS TRIP:

Cultural shock
(Things, People, habits I'm not used to see)

Mood Tracker

Things that make me happy:

Things that make me sad:

Things that make me angry:

Things that make me Calm:

MY TAKEAWAY

OF THIS TRIP IS:

I HAVE LEARNED...

FOR NEXT TRIP I WOULD AVOID...

WHAT I LIKED THE MOST...

COUNTRIES I HAVE VISITED IN MY LIFE...

(TO FILL IN)

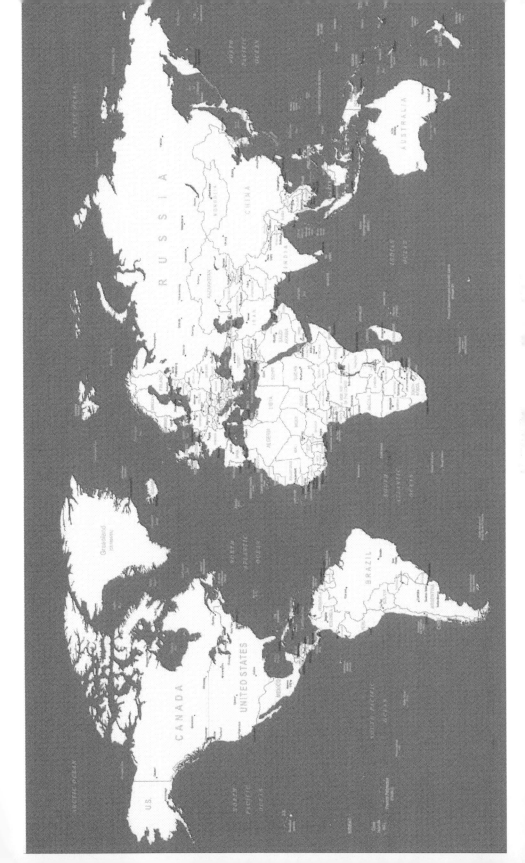

MY BEST PHOTOS

WHEN?

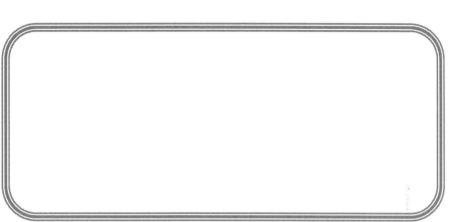

WHERE?

WHEN?

WHERE?

WHEN?

WHERE?

WHEN?

WHERE?

WONDERFUL PEOPLE I MET ON THIS TRIP

NAME:

EMAIL:

COUNTRY:

HE / SHE MADE MY TRIP SPECIAL

BECAUSE...

NAME:

EMAIL:

COUNTRY:

HE / SHE MADE MY TRIP SPECIAL

BECAUSE...

NAME:

EMAIL:

COUNTRY:

HE / SHE MADE MY TRIP SPECIAL

BECAUSE...

NAME:

EMAIL:

COUNTRY:

HE / SHE MADE MY TRIP SPECIAL

BECAUSE...

MY THOUGHTS

My creative space

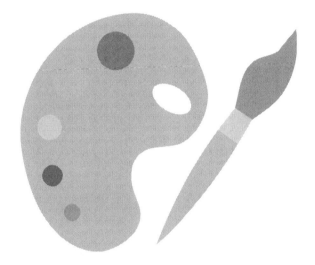

Thanks for leaving a review for this book in Amazon

or sending us your feedback to:

contact@wanderlust-journals.com and get a

40% discount for your next journal.

Don´t forget to visit

The Wanderlust Journals collection

WWW.WANDERLUST-JOURNALS.COM

Printed in Great Britain
by Amazon

76795263R00066